THE 12 MOST INFLUENTIAL
ATHLETES OF ALL TIME

by Jeanne Marie Ford

12 STORY LIBRARY

www.12StoryLibrary.com

12-Story Library is an imprint of Bookstaves and Press Room Editions

Produced for 12-Story Library by Red Line Editorial

Photographs ©: AP Images, cover, 1, 8; Harris & Ewing Collection/Library of Congress, 4; The Arbutus/Indiana University, 5; AP Images, 6; Jim Kerlin/AP Images, 7; Kaliva/Shutterstock Images, 9, 29; Bob Sandberg/Look Magazine Photograph Collection/Library of Congress, 10; Ffooter/Shutterstock Images, 11; Dan Grossi/AP Images, 12; Ira Rosenberg/New York World-Telegram and the Sun Newspaper Photograph Collection/Library of Congress, 13; Suzanne Vlamis/AP Images, 14; Leonard Zhukovsky/Shutterstock Images, 15; Al Messerschmidt/AP Images, 16; stockelements/iStockphoto, 17; Ben Liebenberg/AP Images, 18; Aspen Photo/Shutterstock Images, 19; Kevork Djansezian/AP Images, 20; Dennis Sabo/Shutterstock Images, 21; Leonard Zhukovsky/Shutterstock Images, 22, 23, 28; Desmond Boylan/EPA/Newscom, 24; Antonio Diaz/Shutterstock Images, 25; Kyodo/AP Images, 26; Leonard Zhukovsky/Shutterstock Images, 27

Library of Congress Cataloging-in-Publication Data
Names: Ford, Jeanne Marie, 1971- author.
Title: The 12 Most Influential Athletes of All Time / by Jeanne Marie Ford.
Other titles: Twelve Most Influential Athletes of All Time
Description: Mankato, Minnesota : 12 Story Library, 2018. | Series: The Most
   Influential | Includes bibliographical references and index. | Audience:
   Grade 4 to 6.
Identifiers: LCCN 2016047348 (print) | LCCN 2016053837 (ebook) | ISBN
   9781632354075 (hardcover : alk. paper) | ISBN 9781632354785 (pbk. : alk.
   paper) | ISBN 9781621435303 (hosted e-book)
Subjects: LCSH: Athletes--Biography--Juvenile literature. | Olympic
   athletes--Biography--Juvenile literature. | Sports--History--Juvenile
   literature.
Classification: LCC GV697.A1 F66 2018 (print) | LCC GV697.A1 (ebook) | DDC
   796.092/2--dc23
LC record available at https://lccn.loc.gov/2016047348

Printed in the United States of America
022017

Access free, up-to-date content on this topic plus a full digital version of this book. Scan the QR code on page 31 or use your school's login at 12StoryLibrary.com.

Table of Contents

Jim Thorpe Chases Greatness

Jim Thorpe was one of the world's best all-around athletes. He was born in 1888 in present-day Oklahoma. Thorpe was an American Indian of Sac and Fox descent. Thorpe was a natural athlete. He was fast, powerful, and focused. Thorpe played football and minor league baseball.

In 1912, Thorpe competed in the Olympics in Sweden. He won gold medals in the decathlon and the pentathlon. It was an amazing feat. The king of Sweden called Thorpe the world's greatest athlete. Americans welcomed him home as a hero.

The glory Thorpe had found did not last long. Olympic officials soon took away his medals. He had broken the rules by earning money as a minor-league baseball player. At that time, the Olympics were for amateur athletes only. Critics argued officials had applied the rule unfairly because they did not want an American Indian to win.

Thorpe was a two-time All-American in football at the Carlisle Indian Industrial School.

THE DECATHLON AND PENTATHLON

The 1912 Olympics had two new events, the decathlon and the pentathlon. Both events tested an athlete's strength and stamina over multiple days. The decathlon had ten events. They included sprinting, long-distance running, jumping, hurdles, and throwing. The pentathlon had five events. They were shooting, swimming, fencing, running, and horseback riding.

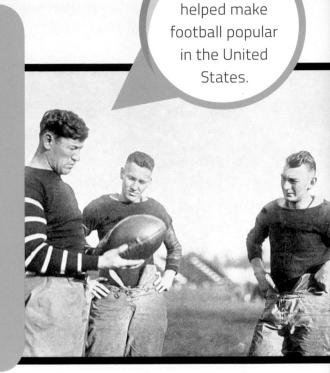

Jim Thorpe helped make football popular in the United States.

After the Olympics, Thorpe returned to baseball. He played as an outfielder for several teams. Then in 1915, Thorpe began to play professional football for the Canton Bulldogs. He was one of the sport's earliest leaders. He retired in 1928.

Thorpe had a lasting impact on the sports world. He helped found the American Professional Football Association, which later became the National Football League (NFL), and served as its first president. In 1963, Thorpe was inducted into the Pro Football Hall of Fame.

In 1999, Thorpe finished third on an Associated Press list of the top athletes of the century.

1983
Year Olympic officials returned Thorpe's gold medals to his family.

- Jim Thorpe won Olympic gold medals in the decathlon and pentathlon.
- Thorpe played professional baseball and football.
- He was one of the century's top athletes.

Babe Didrikson Zaharias Does It All

Mildred Ella Didrikson, later known as Babe Didrikson, was born in 1911. Didrikson was good at every sport she tried. Basketball, baseball, track and field, and swimming all came easily to her. There was a problem, though. Didrikson lived at a time when many people didn't think women should play sports.

Didrikson continued to play sports even though female athletes had limited opportunities to do so. Her goal was to be the best athlete in history. In the 1932 Olympic Games, Didrikson competed in three track and field events. She won gold medals in the javelin throw and 80-meter hurdles. She also won a silver medal in the high jump.

Babe Didrikson broke the world record in the 80-meter hurdles at the 1932 Olympics.

12

Number of strokes by which Babe Didrikson Zaharias won the US Open in 1954.

- Didrikson Zaharias excelled in many sports.
- She helped found the LPGA.
- She was a role model for future female athletes.

Though she had proven her skill, Didrikson faced critics. She didn't fit long-held views of what a lady should be. Many people thought Didrikson and other female athletes should quit.

Didrikson ignored the criticism. After the Olympics, she became a professional athlete. She excelled in bowling, tennis, baseball, softball, and diving. In 1938, Didrikson married wrestler George Zaharias. She also began playing golf. In 1946, she won 13 golf tournaments in a row. A year later, she became the first American golfer to win the British Ladies Amateur.

Babe Didrikson Zaharias was the first woman to play in a PGA Tour event.

As her fame grew, Didrikson Zaharias helped the sport of golf. She helped form the Ladies Professional Golf Association (LPGA) in 1949. Didrikson Zaharias died of cancer just seven years later. Today, her legacy continues. Her courage and athletic skill made the public pay attention to female athletes. As a result, she blazed a path for all future female athletes.

Jesse Owens Races to Victory

Track athlete Jesse Owens was born in 1913 in Alabama. He was the grandson of slaves and the son of sharecroppers. Owens joined his school's track team. By his senior year, Owens had set high school world records in the 100-yard dash, 200-yard dash, and long jump.

Owens went to college at Ohio State. In May 1935, he competed for his school in the Big Ten track championship. At the meet, he broke three world records. He also tied a fourth world record.

For 20 years, Jesse Owens held the Olympic record for the 200-meter dash.

3

Number of records tied or set by Jesse Owens at the 1936 Olympics.

- Jesse Owens won four gold medals in track and field in the 1936 Olympics.
- Owens publicly proved Hitler wrong in the idea that white athletes were superior.
- He paved the way for future black athletes.

THE FASTEST MAN IN THE WORLD

Jamaican sprinter Usain Bolt is known as the fastest man in the world. Bolt won eight gold medals over three Olympic games. He is also the first man to win the 100-meter dash in three Olympics in a row. He has brought excitement to the sport of track and forced his competitors to run faster.

He did all of this in the span of approximately 45 minutes. By the year's end, he had won all 42 events in which he had competed.

Owens wanted to run in the 1936 Olympics. That year, the games were held in Berlin, Germany. Adolf Hitler, Germany's leader, wanted to use the games to prove white people were superior. This made people across the world uneasy about the games.

Despite this, Owens and 17 other black athletes competed for the United States.

Owens won gold medals in four events. It was the first time a US track and field athlete had ever won that many medals at once. Owens had also publicly proven Hitler wrong. His courage and skill paved the way for black athletes who came after him.

As a teenager, Usain Bolt earned the nickname "Lightning Bolt" because of his speed.

Jackie Robinson Shatters Barriers

Baseball great Jackie Robinson was born in Georgia in 1919. He grew up in California, where he was known for being a good athlete. In college, he ran track. He also played football, basketball, and baseball.

In 1945, Robinson began playing baseball in the Negro Leagues. A year later, Branch Rickey presented Robinson with an opportunity.

Rickey was the president of the Brooklyn Dodgers. He asked Robinson to play for his team. Major League Baseball (MLB) had excluded black players since 1900. If Robinson joined the Dodgers, he would be the first.

Robinson accepted Rickey's offer. He played his first major-league game on April 15, 1947. It was a great season for Robinson. He was named Rookie of the Year. Two years later, he was the National League's Most Valuable Player (MVP) and was its batting champion. He went on to lead his team to six pennants and a World Series win in 1955.

Despite his skill, many white people didn't think Robinson should be there. Some Dodgers did not want to have a black player on their team. Some players on other teams felt

Jackie Robinson's record-breaking career earned him a spot in the Baseball Hall of Fame.

Jackie Robinson's retired number at Citi Field in New York

this way, too. Pitchers tried to hit him with the ball. When sliding onto a base, players would step on him with their cleats on purpose. Some fans shouted insults.

In 1997, MLB honored the 50th anniversary of Robinson's first game. His jersey, number 42, was retired by all major-league teams. Today, April 15 is Jackie Robinson Day in baseball. All players and coaches wear number 42. The day honors Robinson's skills as an athlete and his role in ending segregation.

1,518
Number of hits in Jackie Robinson's major-league career.

- Jackie Robinson started his baseball career in the Negro Leagues.
- Robinson was the first black player in Major League.
- He played his entire MLB career with the Brooklyn Dodgers.

BASEBALL'S IRONMEN

Lou Gehrig played an astonishing 2,130 games in a row for the New York Yankees. His consecutive-game record stood for almost 60 years. In 1995, it was broken by Cal Ripken Jr. of the Baltimore Orioles. Ripken played 2,632 games in a row. Both men were called Ironmen for their strength and dedication to the game.

Muhammad Ali Fights His Way to Fame

Cassius Clay was born in Kentucky in 1942. When he was 12 years old, his bike was stolen. That day, he decided he would not be a victim again. He learned how to fight. He began training as a boxer. Six weeks later, he won his first boxing match.

Clay continued to train. In 1960, he joined the US Olympic team and won a gold medal in boxing. Soon afterward, Clay turned pro. In 1964, he knocked out Sonny Liston to win the world heavyweight championship.

Muhammad Ali's career boxing record was 56 wins and 5 losses with 37 knockouts.

31

Number of professional wins Ali had before losing a single match.

- Muhammad Ali was one of the greatest heavyweight boxers.
- Ali fought for racial equality.
- Ali was one of the first public figures to speak out against the Vietnam War.

Two days later, Clay announced his conversion to Islam. His new Muslim name was Muhammad Ali. Ali continued boxing until 1967. That April, he refused to enter the draft for the Vietnam War. He cited his religious beliefs as the reason. The decision cost him dearly. He faced five years in jail for evading the military draft. He also was stripped of all of his boxing titles and was banned from fighting. He spent this time raising awareness about civil rights.

> Muhammad Ali's stance on the Vietnam War and civil rights brought him into politics like no other athlete before him.

In 1971, Ali was cleared of all charges and allowed to return to boxing. During his career, Ali won the heavyweight title three times. He defended the title 19 times. Ali's life and influence outside the ring had been equally important. His stand against the Vietnam War and civil rights influenced the nation.

6

Nadia Comaneci Scores Perfect Tens

Nadia Comaneci was born in 1961 in Romania. At age six, she began training as a gymnast. At that time, gymnastics routines were much simpler than today. They had fewer difficult skills. Routines emphasized grace, dance, and turns.

When Comaneci was 14, she competed at the 1976 Olympics. She displayed daring new skills, especially on the uneven bars. She let go of the bar, somersaulted in

A perfect routine and daring dismount on the uneven bars made Nadia Comaneci a gymnastics legend.

the air, and caught the same bar again. It was the first release move ever performed in competition. Her dismount was also difficult. She swung around the high bar in a pike position. Then she released the bar, doing a half turn into a somersault before landing.

The Olympic judges rewarded Comaneci's skills. They gave her a 10. It was the highest score possible. No one had ever earned a 10 at the Olympics before. The scoreboard did not even have space for all the digits. It showed Comaneci's score as "1.0" instead of "10."

The 1976 Olympics had been a huge success for Comaneci. She had earned a total of seven perfect scores and three gold medals.

9
Number of Olympic medals Nadia Comaneci won in her career.

- Comaneci earned the first perfect score in Olympic gymnastics history.
- Her skills led to a more athletic style of gymnastics.
- Her Olympic performance increased the popularity of the sport.

She had also changed gymnastics forever. Other gymnasts copied Comaneci's skills and built on them. Gymnasts are now rewarded for difficult routines. As a result, the sport's scoring system changed in 1993. There is no more perfect 10.

Simone Biles and other gymnasts have built upon Comaneci's skills.

Michael Jordan Flies High

Michael Jordan was born in 1963 and grew up in North Carolina. He enjoyed playing baseball and basketball as a child. In 10th grade, Jordan was cut from his high school basketball team. It motivated him to practice harder. During this time, he also grew much taller. By the next year, he was his team's star player.

Michael Jordan was voted the NBA's MVP five times.

After high school, Jordan played basketball for the University of North Carolina. In 1984, the Chicago Bulls drafted him. He was an outstanding defensive player and a great shooter.

THINK ABOUT IT

What makes an athlete great? How do you begin to compare a shooting guard and a boxer, a goalie and a pitcher, or a gymnast and a triathlete?

13

Number of career All-Star appearances by Michael Jordan.

- Jordan earned the nickname Air Jordan for his amazing jumps.
- Jordan averaged more than 30 points per game.
- He helped spread the popularity of basketball across the globe.

He was best known for gravity-defying jumps to dunk the ball. This move earned him the nickname Air Jordan.

Jordan retired in 1999. During his career, he led the Bulls to six National Basketball Association (NBA) championships. He led the NBA in scoring in 10 different seasons.

He also earned two Olympic gold medals while on the US basketball team.

Many consider Jordan the greatest basketball player of all time. He helped make professional basketball more popular in the United States and Europe. Current NBA players still study his moves and try to copy them. Even players too young to have watched him play wear Air Jordan sneakers on the court.

Nike began selling Air Jordan sneakers in 1985.

Peyton Manning Rewrites the Record Books

Peyton Manning was born in 1976 into a football family. His father, Archie, played NFL quarterback for 14 seasons. Manning was a competitive athlete from an early age. He and his younger brother, Eli, seemed destined to take after their father.

Peyton was his high school's star quarterback. He earned a scholarship to the University of Tennessee, where he set 42 college records. In 1998, the Indianapolis Colts selected him first overall in the NFL Draft. Manning started every game for the Colts from 1998 through 2010. After missing a year with a neck injury, he joined the Denver Broncos. He played four seasons in Denver before retiring at age 39.

Peyton Manning led the Denver Broncos to a Super Bowl victory in his final NFL game.

71,940

Total career passing yards for Peyton Manning, a record through 2016.

- Manning was one of the most successful quarterbacks in NFL history.
- He led both the Colts and the Broncos to Super Bowl wins.
- Manning retired with career and single-season records for passing yards and touchdown passes.

Many people consider Manning the NFL's best quarterback ever. In his career, he won five MVP awards. He led his teams to two Super Bowl wins. Manning was also one of only two quarterbacks ever to beat all 32 teams in the NFL.

MANNING VS. BRADY

Two of the most successful quarterbacks of all time were Peyton Manning and Tom Brady of the New England Patriots. They played against each other 17 times. Brady won 11 of these match-ups to Manning's six. Four times, they met in the AFC Championship Game. Manning's team won three of those games.

In his career, Manning set many NFL records. He retired holding the records for career passing touchdowns and yards. He also held single-season records for yards and touchdowns.

Peyton Manning's record-breaking career has motivated many young quarterbacks.

19

Mia Hamm Kicks Soccer into the Spotlight

Soccer superstar Mariel "Mia" Hamm was born in 1972. Her father was an Air Force pilot, and she and her five siblings moved often. When Hamm was two, her family was living in Italy. She saw some kids playing soccer and joined them. Her love for soccer had begun.

As her family moved from place to place, Hamm continued to play soccer. She was a natural athlete with a drive to win. Her hard work on the soccer field paid off when she was 15. That year, she became the youngest player on the US women's national soccer team.

From that point on, Hamm's career took off. She led her soccer team at the University of North Carolina to four championships. Then Hamm joined the US women's national team. She helped the team win the World Cup in 1991 and 1999. Hamm also won gold medals for the United States at the Olympics in 1996 and 2004.

In 2012, ESPN named Hamm the best female athlete of the past 40 years.

14

Years Mia Hamm held the record for international soccer goals scored.

- Hamm won two World Cups and two Olympic gold medals.
- Hamm helped found the first women's professional soccer league in the United States.
- She also started a foundation that encourages girls to play sports.

Mia Hamm inspired many girls to play soccer.

Hamm retired in 2004. She had scored 158 international goals. It was the record for any male or female player.

Hamm's skills as a soccer player had drawn attention to the game. People who had never followed soccer before began watching games. Building on this excitement, Hamm became one of the founding members of the first US professional soccer league for women in 2001. It lasted for three seasons before folding.

Today, Hamm's influence continues. She runs the Mia Hamm Foundation. One of its goals is to create more opportunities for girls to play sports.

TITLE IX

The same year Mia Hamm was born, a US law known as Title IX was passed. It required public schools and colleges to fund boys' and girls' activities equally. Before this law, only 1 out of every 27 girls played high school sports. Title IX provided many more opportunities for women to participate in sports and receive scholarships.

10

Serena Williams Overpowers the Competition

Tennis legend Serena Williams was born in 1981. She and her sister Venus grew up in Compton, California. The city had few black athletes who played tennis. But Williams's father wanted his daughters to learn. He began training Serena when she was only four.

The sisters practiced tennis several hours a day. Serena began to develop her own style of tennis. She was fast, moving across the court in a blur. She also had amazingly powerful forehand and backhand strokes. Her average serve sailed across the net at 98 miles per hour (158 km/h). This was a whole new way to play women's tennis.

In 1995, Williams turned professional at the age of 14. At first, she got a lot of attention because of her sister Venus. In singles, the Williams sisters often competed against each other.

Serena Williams at the 2016 Summer Olympics.

In doubles, they played as successful partners.

In 1999, Serena Williams won the US Open. It was her first major title win. The four major titles are called the Grand Slam. In 2002 and 2003, she won five Grand Slam events. By 2016, Williams had won 22 titles in Grand Slam competitions. She had also won four Olympic gold medals.

Tall and muscular, Serena brought power to women's tennis. That was not her only influence on the sport. She also became a face for black female tennis players. In the past, tennis players were typically white.

128

Speed, in miles per hour (206 km/h), of Serena Williams's fastest serve.

- As of 2016, Serena Williams had won 22 Grand Slam titles and four Olympic gold medals.
- Serena is known for her powerful style of play.
- She and her sister Venus have inspired many younger black players to take up the sport.

Serena and Venus Williams have inspired many younger black athletes to take up the sport.

Serena (left) and Venus Williams are rivals, teammates, and sisters who transformed women's tennis.

Misty Copeland Dances Her Way to the Top

Ballet star Misty Copeland was born in 1982 and grew up in California. Her family had little money and moved often. When Copeland was in middle school, she joined the drill team. It was her first experience with dance. The coach noticed Copeland's natural talent. She encouraged Copeland to take ballet classes.

Starting to learn ballet in middle school was late compared to other dancers. But Copeland's ballet teacher encouraged her to continue. Copeland performed at dance competitions in the ballet category. She also won several scholarships for summer dance programs at well-respected dance schools.

As her lessons continued, Copeland improved quickly. In 2001, she joined the corps de ballet at the American Ballet Theatre (ABT). Out of 80 dancers in the corps, she was the only black person.

Copeland began to advance to higher positions at the ABT. In 2007, she became a soloist. It was only the second time in 20 years that a black person had been in that role for the ABT.

Misty Copeland challenged the idea of what a ballerina looks like.

Misty Copeland is a role model to a new generation of ballet dancers.

In 2015, Copeland reached the high point of her career. She was named the principal dancer of the ABT. She was the first black female to have this position in ABT's 75-year history. As the principal dancer, Copeland receives the leading female roles in ABT's ballets.

Copeland's success has changed people's image of the ideal ballerina. In the past, ballerinas were usually white and thin. Copeland is black and has a curvy, muscular build. Copeland has brought a new sense of excitement to ballet, too. She shared her experience with ballet in her book *Life in Motion*.

13
Age Misty Copeland took dance lessons for the first time.

- Copeland has broken barriers by being a curvy, muscular, black ballet dancer.
- She is the first black female principal dancer in the ABT's 75-year history.
- Copeland has generated new excitement about ballet.

THINK ABOUT IT

Dancers are athletes, but most people don't think of dance as a sport. Auto racing is a sport, but most people don't think of drivers as athletes. What makes a person an athlete? What is a sport?

Michael Phelps Swims into the History Books

Michael Phelps is swimming's biggest star. He was born in Maryland in 1985. His older sisters were competitive swimmers. He was always at the pool for their meets. So his parents signed him up for lessons, too.

At age 11, Phelps began training seriously. Just four years later, he was on the US Olympic team.

In 2008, Phelps set a record for winning eight gold medals for swimming in a single Olympics.

Phelps went on to compete in five Olympic Games. He won 28 medals, and 23 of them were gold. This makes Phelps the most decorated Olympic athlete of all time.

As Phelps continued to win medals, more people started to pay attention to swimming. Before Phelps, swimming did not have as many fans as other sports.

- Michael Phelps is the most successful swimmer in Olympic history.
- He competed in five Olympic games.
- He brought new attention to the sport and inspired the next generation of swimmers.

THINK ABOUT IT

Do certain sports require more athletic ability than others? Who do you think is the greatest athlete of all time? Why?

Seeing Phelps win race after race changed that. Suddenly, people were tuning in to cheer on Phelps. It was exciting to see him break records and win gold medals.

Phelps also inspired other swimmers. They watched him shatter world records. They saw him compete in several individual events, not just specialize in one or two. These swimmers pushed themselves and set high goals, just as Phelps had done. By the end of the 2016 Olympics, Phelps had elevated competitive swimming to a new level.

Michael Phelps celebrates his team's victory in the 4x100 meter medley relay in the 2016 Olympic Games.

Other Notable Athletes

Wayne Gretzky

Wayne Gretzky is one of hockey's greatest players. He holds National Hockey League records for goals scored, assists, and total points in a career.

Billie Jean King

Billie Jean King was a professional tennis player who helped organize the Women's Tennis Association. She also showed how skilled female tennis players could be when she beat male opponent Bobby Riggs in a "Battle of the Sexes."

Bruce Lee

Bruce Lee popularized martial arts around the world. He displayed his dazzling skills in competitions and in action movies.

Wilma Rudolph

While still in high school, Wilma Rudolph won a sprint relay medal at the 1956 Olympics. In 1960, she became the first American woman to win three gold medals in track and field at a single Olympic Games.

Deion Sanders

Deion Sanders is one of the few athletes who has played both professional baseball and football. He is the only athlete to have competed in both the Super Bowl and the World Series.

Tiger Woods

Tiger Woods is one of the world's best golfers. He was the youngest winner of the Masters tournament and the first winner who was of African American or Asian ancestry.

Glossary

amateur
An athlete who is not paid to play his or her sport.

corps de ballet
Ballet dancers who perform as a group and do not have solos.

dismount
A move that a gymnast uses to get off the uneven bars or balance beam.

draft
To select a person for a team; to require a person to join the military.

drill team
A dance group that uses sharp, precise movements.

hurdles
A tall frame over which a racer jumps.

javelin
A spear thrown in track and field events.

pike
A position in which the body is bent in half but the legs are straight.

rookie
An athlete who is playing his or her first season.

scholarship
An award of money that helps a student pay for college.

segregation
Separating people based on their skin color or religion.

sharecropper
A farmer who does not own the land he or she works.

For More Information

Books

Editors of Sports Illustrated Kids. *Big Book of Who: The 101 Athletes Every Fan Needs to Know*. New York: Time Home Entertainment, 2014.

Stabler, David. *Kid Athletes: True Tales of Childhood from Sports Legends*. Philadelphia, PA: Quirk Books, 2015.

Tejada, Justin. *Sports Illustrated Kids Stats! The Greatest Numbers in Sports*. New York: Time Home Entertainment, 2013.

Visit 12StoryLibrary.com

Scan the code or use your school's login at **12StoryLibrary.com** for recent updates about this topic and a full digital version of this book. Enjoy free access to:

- Digital ebook
- Breaking news updates
- Live content feeds
- Videos, interactive maps, and graphics
- Additional web resources

Note to educators: Visit 12StoryLibrary.com/register to sign up for free premium website access. Enjoy live content plus a full digital version of every 12-Story Library book you own for every student at your school.

Editor's note: The 12 topics featured in this book are selected by the author and approved by the book's editor. While not a definitive list, the selected topics are an attempt to balance the book's subject with the intended readership. To expand learning about this subject, please visit **12StoryLibrary.com** or use this book's QR code to access free additional content.

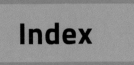

Index

About the Author

Jeanne Marie Ford is an Emmy-winning TV scriptwriter and holds an MFA in Writing for Children from Vermont College. She has written numerous children's books and articles and also teaches college English. She lives in Maryland with her husband and two children.

READ MORE FROM 12-STORY LIBRARY

Every 12-Story Library book is available in many formats. For more information, visit 12StoryLibrary.com.